D0637559

10 Things You Can Do To

Save Water

by Jenny Mason

Content Consultant
Howard Perlman
U.S. Geological Survey

Reading Consultant
Jeanne M. Clidas, Ph.D.
Reading Specialist

Children's Press®
An Imprint of Scholastic Inc.

Table of Contents

We could not live without water. We need fresh water to drink, clean ourselves, and grow our food. But when water appears in your home, it must disappear from somewhere else. If people do not **conserve** fresh water, there will not be enough for everyone. The good news is that you can help. There are lots of ways you can conserve water.

Control the Flow

Turn off the faucet when you brush your teeth or wash your hands. When you do run the water, let it trickle. Do not blast it. You can make your toilet use less water, too. Put a filled-up water bottle in the tank. It will raise the water level. Then the toilet will use less water to refill when you flush.

Water Cycle

condensation

rain and snow

evaporation

surface runoff

groundwater

The amount of water on Earth never changes. That means a dinosaur might have sipped the water you showered in today! Water **evaporates** from the land and ocean into the air. Then it returns to the ground as rain and snow. This is the water cycle.

Turning off the faucet saves water every time you brush!

7

Find and Fix

Leaky toilets can waste 200 gallons (757 liters) of water in a day. Your parents can fix any in your home. You just have to find them first!

Try to picture 200 gallons. That's a lot of water!

Leaky Toilets

Put a few drops of food coloring in the toilet tank. See if the water in the bowl changes color. If it does, the toilet has a silent leak that needs to be fixed.

Almost 90 percent of the ice on Earth is in Antarctica.

The water that flows into our homes is freshwater. This water is safe to drink. (Ocean water is too salty!) Almost 70 percent of all of the freshwater on Earth exists in ice and **glaciers**.

3 Take Showers,

Save bubble baths for a special treat.

One bath uses the same amount of water as three showers. Isn't that amazing? Save water by taking showers instead of

Not Baths

baths. And remember to keep your shower short! That will help conserve water, too.

It takes about 40 gallons (150 liters) of water to fill a bathtub. A five-minute shower uses less than 10 gallons (40 liters). The choice is easy!

Recycle and Reuse

Factories use a lot of water to make different products. Instead of buying new stuff, reuse what you have! And make sure you recycle plastic, paper, and cans. Recycled plastic bottles can be made into backpacks. Aluminum cans can become bikes!

The kids on this team have collected a lot of recyclables.

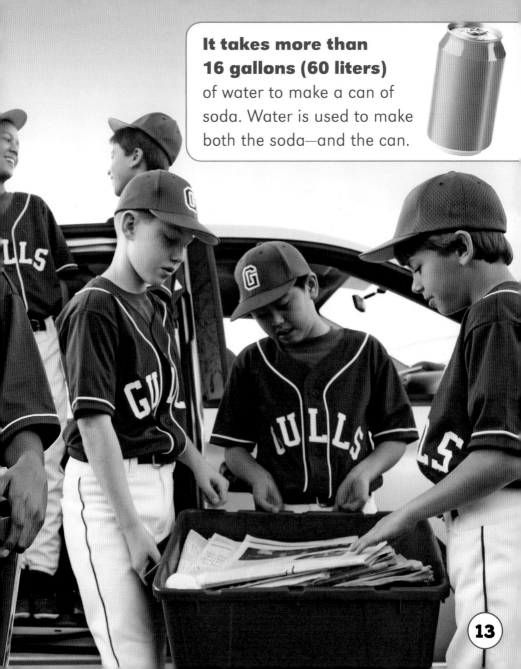

It takes more than 16 gallons (60 liters) of water to make a can of soda. Water is used to make both the soda—and the can.

Use Natural Cleaners

Everything that goes down the drain can end up in our water. Cleaning chemicals can **pollute** rivers, lakes, and seas. This makes water unsafe for people, plants, and animals. Using natural cleaners like baking soda and vinegar can help.

Polluted water is threatening orcas near Seattle, Washington.

Rain also carries chemicals to lakes, rivers, and oceans. That polluted water ruins animal habitats. The creatures that live there get sick. Many even die.

You can put vinegar and
water in a squirt bottle.
Use it to clean windows.

6 Save Water While

Warm water is best for taking showers and washing dishes.
But running the water while it warms up wastes a lot. Do not let the water

Water that would have been wasted is put to good use in the garden.

It Warms

run down the drain. Catch it in a jar at the sink. You can also use a bucket in the shower. Then share that water with plants.

Clouds are made of tiny drops of water. A LOT of tiny drops! The average white cloud weighs more than one million pounds (500,000 kilograms). That is like having 100 elephants overhead!

Build a Rain Garden

Position your garden in a spot where water will run into it after a rainfall. This could be near a driveway or a downspout. Make a shallow hole, and plant deep-rooted plants and grasses. As the water sinks into the garden, it is pulled deep into the ground. There it gets cleaned by the earth.

A rain garden will also add beauty to your yard!

Wetlands work the same way rain gardens do. Water that enters these swamps, marshes, and ponds is cleaned naturally.

A rosebush drinks about 15 gallons (58 liters) of water a week. A birch tree can drink two bathtubs' worth every day! All the grassy lawns in the U.S. guzzle about two very full Lake Meads (right) every year.

8 Learn About Your

A watershed is a big area of land where water collects. The water runs off the land into nearby bodies of water. Without a good watershed, people

Explore your watershed to make sure it is clean and healthy.

Watershed

cannot get enough water. Arrange a trip for your school or club to see your watershed. It will inspire you—and your friends—to conserve water.

An aquifer is an area underground where water fills in the spaces between rocks, clay, sand, and gravel. The Ogallala Aquifer stretches under eight states in the middle of the country. Sadly, even that is not enough water to meet our needs. The Ogallala is drying up!

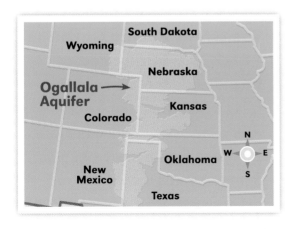

The Ogallala Aquifer is one of the biggest in the world.

Two million tons (1.8 million metric tons) of trash end up in Earth's waters every day. Trash is bad for wildlife—and people. Plan a trip to a local river, lake, or beach. Put on a pair of gloves and pick up the trash, even if you did not leave it there.

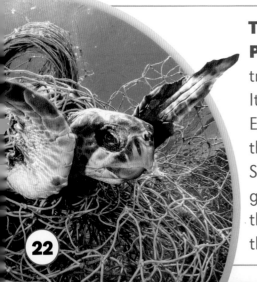

The Great Pacific Garbage Patch is a huge area of trash floating in the ocean. It is twice the size of Texas. Every year, the trash kills more than a million marine animals. Some animals drown because they get tangled up in garbage (like this turtle did). Others die when they mistake the junk for food.

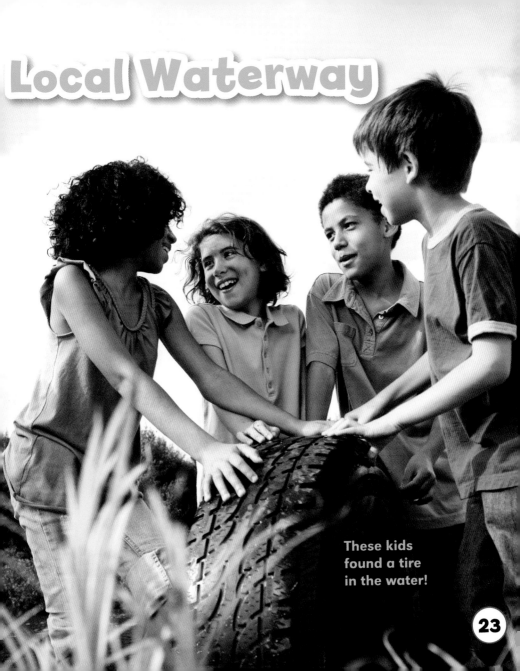

Local Waterway

These kids
found a tire
in the water!

10

Spill the Facts

You have learned so much about water. You know how to keep it clean and how to save it! Now share everything you know with your friends and family. The more people who care about protecting Earth's water, the better off we will be!

Over your lifetime, you will drink as much as 20,000 gallons (76,000 liters) of water. That is enough water to fill a medium-size inground swimming pool!

Cleaning Up: Project

Are you wondering if kids really can make a difference? James Hemphill grew up in Virginia Beach, Virginia. When he was just 11, James noticed a lot of trash piling up along the rivers and on the beach. He knew he had to do something—even if he was just a kid. He asked his friends at school for help. In three years, they removed 6,000 pounds (2,722 kilograms) of trash from a creek near his school. James did not want to stop there. He started a club called Project Green

Green Teens

Teens. The club removed 5,000 pounds (2,268 kilograms) of trash and junk from the beaches in the Chesapeake Bay area. To this day, the club still cleans and protects the local waters.

Be Water Wise!

When you see how little clean water there is to share, you will know why it's so important to conserve it!

There are **326 quintillion** gallons of water on Earth.

3% of the water on Earth is freshwater.

97% of the water on Earth is salt water.

Almost **70%** of all the freshwater on Earth exists in ice and glaciers.

Only **.007%** of the freshwater is clean and drinkable.

4.7 billion people in the world must share all of Earth's freshwater.

1 in 9 people does not have access to clean water.

.25% of the freshwater is in lakes, rivers, and groundwater.

Glossary

conserve (kuhn-SURV): save something from loss, decay, or waste

evaporates (ee-VAP-uh-rayts): changes from a liquid into a vapor or gas

glaciers (GLAY-shurs): slow-moving masses of ice found in mountain valleys or polar regions

pollute (puh-LOOT): contaminate or make dirty

Index

About the Author

Jenny Mason lives in Colorado, near lots of lakes and rivers. Her favorite ways to play in water include fishing, building snowmen, paddleboarding, and swimming.

Facts for Now

Visit this Scholastic Web site for
more information on how to save water:
www.factsfornow.scholastic.com
Enter the keywords **Save Water**

Library of Congress Cataloging-in-Publication Data

Names: Mason, Jenny (Children's author)
Title: 10 things you can do to save water / by Jenny Mason.
Other titles: Ten things you can do to save water
Description: New York, NY : Children's Press, an imprint of Scholastic Inc., [2017] | Series: Rookie star: make a difference | Includes index.
Identifiers: LCCN 2016003484 | ISBN 9780531226513 (library binding) | ISBN 9780531227572 (pbk.)
Subjects: LCSH: Water conservation—Juvenile literature. | Water-supply—Juvenile literature. | Water reuse—Juvenile literature.
Classification: LCC TD348 .M36 2017 | DDC 333.91/16—dc23
LC record available at http://lccn.loc.gov/2016003484

No part of this publication may be reproduced in whole or in part, or stored in a retrieval system, or transmitted in any form or by any means, electronic, mechanical, photocopying, recording, or otherwise, without written permission of the publisher. For information regarding permission, write to Scholastic Inc., Attention: Permissions Department, 557 Broadway, New York, NY 10012.

Produced by Spooky Cheetah Press
Design by Judith Christ-Lafond

© 2017 by Scholastic Inc.

All rights reserved. Published in 2017 by Children's Press, an imprint of Scholastic Inc.

Printed in China 62

SCHOLASTIC, CHILDREN'S PRESS, ROOKIE STAR™ MAKE A DIFFERENCE,
and associated logos are trademarks and/or registered trademarks of Scholastic Inc.

2 3 4 5 6 7 8 9 10 R 25 24 23 22 21 20 19 18 17 16

Photographs ©: cover grass: Anan Kaewkhammul/Shutterstock, Inc.; cover water: stockphoto-graf/Shutterstock, Inc.; cover right surgeonish: Kletr/Shutterstock, Inc.; cover boy: Hero Images Inc./Alamy Images; cover yellow butterflies: kurga/Thinkstock; cover fish bowl: tanuha2001/Shutterstock, Inc.; cover clown fish: bluehand/Shutterstock, Inc.; cover blue fish and red fish: mexrix/Shutterstock, Inc.; cover bottom yellow fish: serg_dibrova/Shutterstock, Inc.; cover left angelfish: serg_dibrova/Shutterstock, Inc.; cover splash: Kubais/Shutterstock, Inc.; cover red butterflies: Cezar Serbanescu/Getty Images; 2 top left: pterwort/Fotolia; 2 top right: Elaine Thompson/AP Images; 2 bottom: robert_s/Shutterstock, Inc.; 3 top: Kuttelvaserova Stuchelova/Shutterstock, Inc.; 3 center: graphego/Shutterstock, Inc.; 3 bottom: robert_s/Shutterstock, Inc.; 4-5 background: Roberto Machado Noa/Getty Images; 5 background: Roberto Machado Noa/Getty Images; 5 top: Juan Carlos Lino/Alamy Images; 5 center: DeeMPhotography/Shutterstock, Inc.; 5 bottom, 6-7: Stephanie Rausser/Getty Images; 7 inset: Kazakova Maryia/Shutterstock, Inc.; 8 left: buyit/Thinkstock; 8 center: SergiyN/Fotolia; 8 right: Ermolaev Alexander/Shutterstock, Inc.; 9 top: Viktor1/Shutterstock, Inc.; 9 bottom: Denis Burdin/Shutterstock, Inc.; 10 left: Svetamart/Dreamstime; 10 right: John Black/Dreamstime; 10-11 background: visivostudio/Shutterstock, Inc.; 10-11 bubbles: Andrey Zametalov/Dreamstime; 11 top: Filipe B. Varela/Shutterstock, Inc.; 11 bottom: Riverlim/Dreamstime; 12-13: Fuse/Thinkstock; 13 inset: fotofermer/Thinkstock; 14: Elaine Thompson/AP Images; 15: Kathleen Finlay/Media Bakery; 16-17 bottom: Lucian Coman/Shutterstock, Inc.; 17 top: sutichak/Fotolia; 18: Bill Coster/Alamy Images; 19 top inset: Chris Findon/Alamy Images; 20: Dmitrii Kiselev/Dreamstime; 21 top: Pirotehnik/Thinkstock; 22: Jordi Chias/Nature Picture Library; 23: Volt Collection/Shutterstock, Inc.; 24-25: Media Bakery; 25 girl: Sam74100/Dreamstime; 25 glass: zozzzzo/Thinkstock; 26-27 : Photo_Concepts/iStockphoto; 28-29 infographic: Brown Bird Design; 30 top: Stephanie Rausser/Getty Images; 30 center top: graphego/Shutterstock, Inc.; 30 center bottom: daboost/Thinkstock; 28-29 infographic: Brown Bird Design; 30 center bottom: Denis Burdin/Shutterstock, Inc.; 30 bottom: Overcrew55/Dreamstime; 30 water: robert_s/Shutterstock, Inc.; 31: robert_s/Shutterstock, Inc.; 32: robert_s/Shutterstock, Inc.

Map by Jim McMahon